JUSTIN BIEBER
HIS WORLD

By Riley Brooks

SCHOLASTIC INC.
New York   Toronto   London   Auckland
Sydney   Mexico City   New Delhi   Hong Kong

© 2010 by Scholastic
ISBN 978-0-545-25357-4

Published by Scholastic Inc.
SCHOLASTIC and associated logos are trademarks and/or registered
trademarks of Scholastic Inc.

12 11 10 9 8 7 6 5   10 11 12 13 14 15/0

Printed in the U.S.A.
First printing, April 2010   40

Table of Contents

Introduction

Have you ever wondered what it would be like to meet Justin Bieber? To watch him sing and dance in front of crowds of screaming fans? Hang with him in the recording studio? Ride along on the bus while he goes on tour? It would be awesome, right?

Well, get ready to find out. This book is packed with all things Justin—from his childhood in Ontario to his recording sessions with Usher to his jam-packed performances. Plus, it has all the facts every Justin fan should know and tons of photos! It's almost as good as being there with J.B.!

Before Justin was an international pop sensation he was just an average boy growing up outside of Ontario, Canada. Little Justin was born on March 1, 1994, to proud parents Pattie Mallette and Jeremy Bieber. They knew right away that there was something special about their son. He was adorable from the start!

Justin's parents got a divorce when Justin was little, but they have both always been supportive of Justin. Justin grew up in a small town called Stratford with his mom. It was a nice, safe town where Justin and his friends could go hiking in the woods, play soccer in the park, and organize hockey games in the winter months. Justin went to elementary and middle school near his home at Downie Central Public School and Avon Public School. He was popular and had a great group of friends growing up, including his best friend, Ryan Butler. Justin was an easygoing kid who loved to be in the spotlight. He excelled in sports—especially hockey. For a long time, he hoped to become a professional hockey player one day, just like his hero Wayne Gretzky. But his mom always had a feeling that music might be Justin's true calling.

When Justin was only two years old, he already started showing musical talent. "I was basically banging on everything I could get my hands on," Justin told reuters.com. Justin's mom saved up money for two years to buy him a drum kit. Justin loved it and taught himself to play the drums fairly quickly. Encouraged by his natural musical abilities, Pattie also bought him a keyboard and a guitar. "I've always loved music, especially percussion. . . . My mom bought me my first drum kit when I was four because I was banging on everything around the house, even couches. I picked up the guitar when I was six and taught myself to play, but I didn't really start singing

until I was ten," Justin explained to reuters.com. Even Pattie was surprised and impressed by just how gifted he was. "When he was five, he'd hear something on the radio and go to the keyboard and figure it out," she explained to *Entertainment Weekly.* It was pretty impressive for a five-year-old who had never taken a music lesson!

Justin was a talented, happy kid, but that didn't mean things were always easy for him. He and his mom struggled to make ends meet. Pattie worked two jobs and studied web design at night, hoping to eventually land a job with better hours and pay. "We were living below the poverty line," Patty told *Entertainment Weekly.* "We had a roof over our heads and we had food in the house, but we really struggled." In the end, though, their struggles were worth it. These days, Pattie owns her own web design company and can spend much more time with her son.

Justin's love of music really took off when he was in seventh grade. Twelve-year-old Justin decided to enter a local singing competition called Stratford Idol. Based on the popular television show *American Idol*, Stratford Idol gave local talents a chance to sing to win a grand prize. Justin decided to enter on a whim, but he faced some stiff and very well-trained competition. "The other people in the competition had been taking singing lessons and had vocal coaches. I wasn't taking it too seriously at the time, I would just sing around the house," Justin explained on justinbiebermusic.com. He didn't even practice before the competition! He just showed up the day of the competition and decided to sing Matchbox Twenty's "3 A.M." "It was nothing huge. I just thought it would be fun," Justin told *Entertainment Weekly*. The judges were blown away by his confident

performance and sweet voice. He won second place.

Justin's family was super proud of his accomplishment. But a few of them hadn't been able to make the show. So Justin posted a video of his performance on YouTube so they could see it. His family members left plenty of encouraging comments. And, to Justin's surprise, so did a lot of other YouTube surfers who stumbled upon his video. Justin

was floored. He never imagined that his video would become so popular. "I was never the kid that was like, 'Oh, I want to be famous.' Or, 'I want to be out there.' Not at all, really. I sang, but it was just for fun. . . . I did a lot of different stuff. I played sports. Singing was just another hobby. . . . And I never took it seriously. I never got lessons. I used to practice my signature for hockey. It's kind of how I learned to give my autograph," Justin told *The Toronto Sun*. Soon his fans were clamoring for more Justin videos. So Justin began videotaping himself performing covers of his favorite songs by artists like Usher, Ne-Yo, and Stevie Wonder, and posting them on YouTube. Before long, Justin's videos had logged over fifty-five million views. It was a huge following and music pros began taking notice.

Scooter Braun, a music manager with a reputation for spotting fresh talent, was intrigued by Justin's videos. It took some investigating, but eventually Scooter managed to get Justin's contact information. "He was very, very persistent," Justin explained to reuters.com. "He even called my great-aunt and my school board." Scooter convinced Justin to seriously consider a singing career. Justin signed with Scooter, but he still wasn't sure anything could come of it. In fact, Justin didn't even tell his friends what was going on! "I didn't tell my friends because they didn't really know that I could sing. They knew me for playing sports. I just wanted to be a regular kid, and I knew they wouldn't treat me the same way if I told them," Justin explained to reuters.com. Justin didn't know it at the time, but he would never really be a regular kid again. He was already on the road to becoming a pop super-star!

Scooter didn't waste any time building exposure in the music world for thirteen-year-old Justin. He knew that artists well known for their smooth blends of pop music and R&B would be very interested in his new protégé. Scooter targeted stars like Usher and Justin Timberlake who had their own labels. First up, they flew down to Atlanta, Georgia, so that Justin could sing for Island Def Jam Records' CEO, Antonio "L.A." Reid. Usher, one of Justin's musical idols and a part of Island Def Jam, happened to be recording in Atlanta at the time. Justin got the chance to meet him, although it didn't go quite as well as Justin had hoped, as he explained to mtv.com: "Usher happens to roll up in his Range Rover, so I was like, 'Man, that's Usher.' So I ran up to him." Justin told the singer how much he loved his music and asked if he could sing a song for

Usher. But Usher didn't know who Justin was
then and wasn't interested in hearing him sing
at the time.

However, a week or so later Usher watched
Justin's videos and immediately regretted his
decision. "He actually watched my videos
and was like, 'Man, I should have let this kid

sing,'" Justin told mtv.com. "And he flew me back to Atlanta. I got to sing for him, and then a week later, I had a meeting with Justin Timberlake. They both kind of wanted me."

They did indeed. Justin Timberlake and Usher both wanted to sign Justin Bieber to a big-time record deal. It was a difficult decision for a thirteen-year-old boy to make! Luckily, Justin had his mom and his manager to give him great advice and help him make the right choice. He eventually decided to go with Usher and signed his record deal with Island Def Jam Records and RBMG.

Usher and everyone at Island Def Jam were thrilled. "He was an amazing talent and find. Given my experience, I knew exactly what it would take for him to become an incredible artist," Usher told reuters.com. Like Justin, Usher signed his first record deal at age

thirteen, so he knew just how to guide the young star. "He [Usher] just basically told me to keep my head on straight. Make sure to stay grounded. I mean, he's been through the whole process. He's done it all before so he's kind of coaching me. He's kind of my mentor," Justin explained to neonlimelight.com. As a good mentor, Usher helped Justin gather together a great collection of songs and got him into the recording studio to work on his first album as soon as possible.

Justin knew exactly what type of album he would like to put out. He wanted his sound to be a smooth blend of catchy pop and groovy R&B. And he wanted to sing about what he knew—puppy love, teen life, and having fun with his friends. He was planning to call the album *My World.* Usher knew exactly how to achieve that, especially given Justin's natural talents. He and Justin selected songs from incredible writers and recorded them with the help of some of the top producers in the music industry. Justin even helped write one of the songs! "Most [of the songs on *My World*] are about love and stuff that girls can appreciate, but I also co-wrote a song called 'Down to Earth.' It's a ballad about the feelings I had when my parents split up and how I helped my family get through it. I think a lot of kids have had their parents split up, and they should know that it wasn't because of something they did. I hope people can relate to it," Justin explained to reuters.com.

Justin threw himself into recording with serious passion and commitment. Usher even joined Justin on "First Dance," a song that Justin described on justinbieber.com as: "a slow, groovy song that people can dance to." Justin wanted his record to be perfect and he pushed himself to excel more than Usher ever pushed Justin! "Well, I mean, I'm kind of a perfectionist, so I always like to do my best. Yeah . . . I guess there's a little bit of pressure, but I don't think he [Usher] puts that on me. I think that it's just me," Justin explained to neonlimelight.com. The result was better than Justin could ever have hoped.

My World was everything Justin wanted it to be. "There's a lot of stuff that's not just about love. There's songs that teens can relate to, as far as parents not being together and divorce. And just stuff that happens in everyday life. There's a lot of kids [stars] my age [and] their whole album [is] 'Everything is perfect.' Real life isn't perfect, so my album kind of portrays that. You just have to make the best of what you have," Justin told mtv.com. Everyone who heard the finished record was impressed. "People don't hear it and think, 'Oh, it's a little kid's record,'" Scooter, Justin's manager, told reuters.com. "He's a young kid who sings with a lot more soul than he should."

Justin's first single was the catchy "One Time." It was produced by rapper Tricky and it was all about puppy love, one of Justin's favorite topics. As soon as the single was released on July 7, 2009, Justin fans began clamoring to hear it on the radio and down-

loading it. It went platinum in his home country of Canada a few months later. "One Time" was followed by three other singles before the official album release: "One Less Lonely Girl," "Love Me," and "Favorite Girl." All four singles were Top 15 hits in Canada and Top 40 hits in the United States. That was a very big deal in the music industry. In fact, Justin is the only artist in history to have four singles from a debut album in the Top 40 before the album's release. So when *My World* finally hit store shelves on November 17, 2009, it was no surprise that it was an immediate hit!

To promote his debut album, Justin recorded videos for some of his singles. You'd think Justin would have already been a video pro since his career started on YouTube, but making a professional music video was a big change! "It was really different going from a video camera to a professional camera. It was really crazy, but it was an amazing experience," Justin explained to billboard.com.

Usher made a cameo in the video for "One Time" when he asks Justin to watch his house for him for a while. Justin agrees and then throws a huge house party to try to get close to his crush. Usher catches him in the middle of the party at the end of the video, but somehow you can't imagine anyone as cute as Justin getting into any real trouble with his mentor! Justin loved filming with Usher on the set, as he explained to neonlimelight.com: "He's just

a regular cat like you and me, so it's just like hanging out with anybody else. But it's cool. It's cool to have one of my inspirations on set."

Of course, the best part of filming was getting to flirt with his beautiful costars! Justin filmed videos for "One Time" and "One Less Lonely Girl" in 2009. Since both songs are about falling in love, Justin had to have beautiful girls to sing to in the videos. Filming was serious work, but it was also a lot of fun to have kids his own age on set to hang out with. The end results were fantastic—fans loved the videos and they gave Justin's singles a lot of exposure.

CHAPTER 6

Justin's World

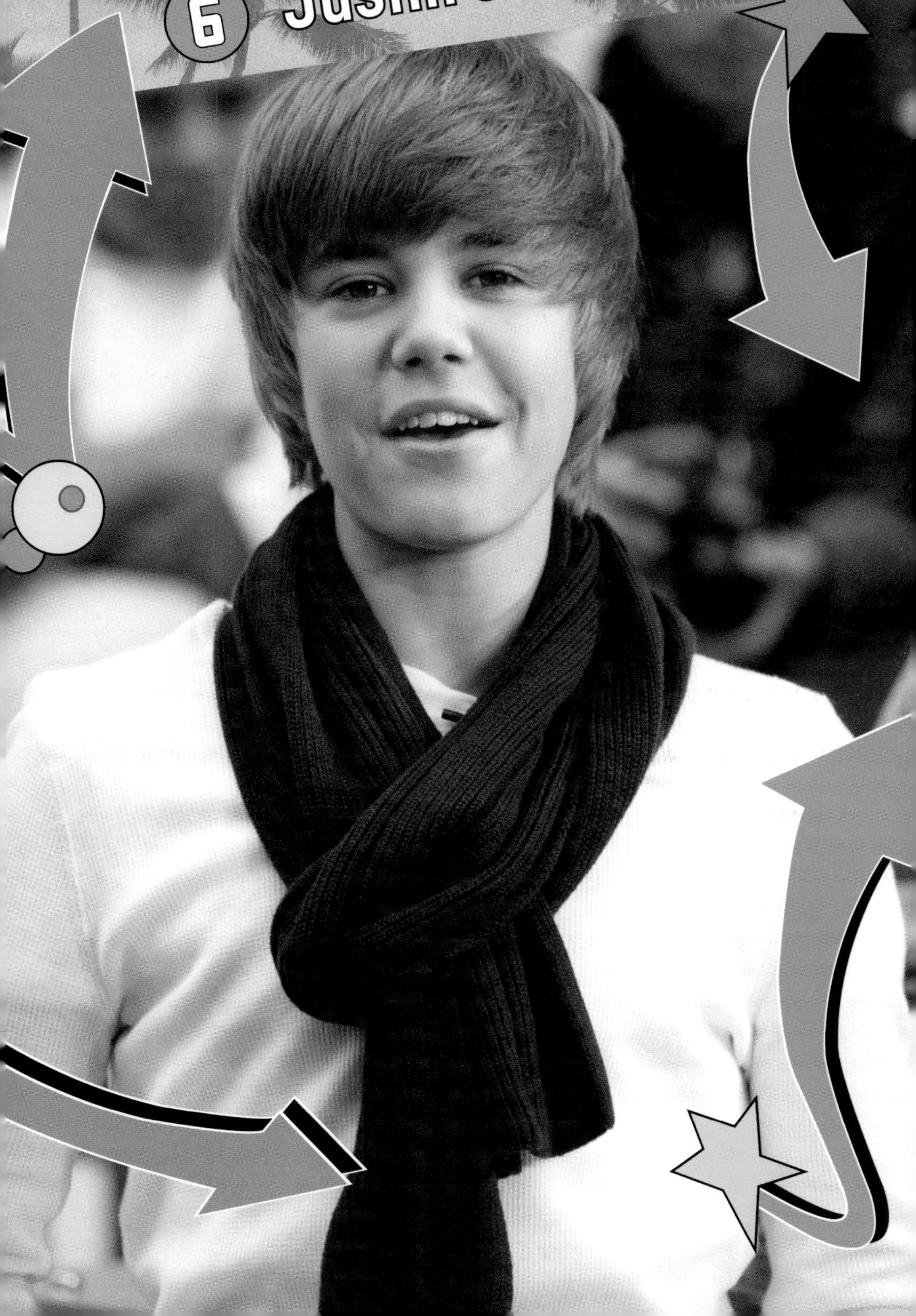

With the release of *My World*, Justin officially became a household name that no one could ignore. His videos and singles had already been rising steadily in popularity, but the blitz of media exposure surrounding his album release really put Justin on the map. He gave thousands of interviews, appeared on popular TV shows and blogs, and began tweeting regularly to keep his fans in the loop. "I think the Internet is the best way to reach your fans. A couple of years back, artists didn't have that tool, so why not use it now? I'm also on Facebook, and my fans got together and sent me a 'get well' card on Twitter when I was sick the other day. That was really cool," Justin told reuters.com.

When Justin appeared on NBC's *Today Show*, filmed at New York City's Rockefeller Plaza, more than two thousand fans came out at the crack of dawn for the performance. It was the largest crowd for any artist in 2009! Justin was also invited to introduce country teen superstar Taylor Swift's performance at the 2009 MTV Video Music Awards alongside Nickelodeon actress Miranda Cosgrove. After an embarrassing moment earlier at the awards show when Kanye West stormed the stage and insinuated that Taylor Swift did not deserve her award for best female video of the year, Justin knew he had to play it just right. He walked out onto the stage and said, "First of all, I'd just like to say give it up for Taylor Swift. She deserved that award." It wasn't in the script—but it was just what the crowd needed to hear. It also forged a friendship between Justin and Taylor that is still going strong today. "After I presented, Taylor Swift thanked me for saying that she deserved to win her award. She said, 'Thanks for sticking up for me, lil' bro,' and I was like, 'Yeah, I've got your back,'" Justin explained to reuters.com.

Justin has made a lot of other amazing celebrity friendships since launching his album, including one of his idols, P. Diddy! And Justin told *The Toronto Sun* that he wasn't shy about flirting with a singer much older than he is: "We were at a dinner and I was like, 'It would be funny if I asked Rihanna out.' And I did just for fun. She said no. I wasn't expecting her to say yes." But his favorite part about stardom is getting to meet and inspire his fans. "I'm looking forward to influencing others in a positive way," Justin explained on justinbiebermusic.com. "My message is you can do anything if you just put your mind to it. I grew up below the poverty line; I didn't have as much as other people did. I think it made me stronger as a person; it built my character. Now I have a 4.0 grade point average and I want to go to college and just become a better person." Justin's success is definitely inspiring his fans around the world!

So what's life like behind the scenes for pop's fastest-rising star? Well, it's a lot busier than it used to be! These days Justin and his mom call Atlanta, Georgia, home. They moved down from Ontario so that Justin could be closer to Usher while recording his album. It's been a big change! "In my town [in Canada], there were only thirty thousand people, but in Atlanta there are millions," Justin told *MTV News.* "And I don't know anybody [in Atlanta], but everybody knows everybody in my town in Canada." Justin definitely misses being close to his father and, of course, all of his friends and classmates. But he keeps in touch with plenty of calls, e-mails, and trips. "I've been traveling so much I haven't got back to Stratford in a while," Justin told *The Toronto Sun.* "And when I go back I'm like, there for a day, and then I leave again." Missing quality time with his old friends, Justin invited

his best friend to join him in his "One Time" video. It was a great way to share his success with his bud.

School is a lot different these days as well. Justin is officially enrolled in the School of Young Performers in New York City. The school was designed just for kids like Justin! He does his schoolwork on the road with a tutor. It's been great for Justin to be able to do his work at his own pace, and he currently maintains his perfect 4.0 G.P.A.

So does Justin miss big school moments like pep rallies, dances, and prom? Nah! He's got plenty of amazing events to attend for his music career that are just as fun. He does miss getting to flirt with girls at school though. It's much harder to meet and get to know girls these days. He meets lots of gorgeous fans, but signing autographs doesn't really count as

quality time! All of Justin's fans want to know if he has a girlfriend. Good news—he's single! "I haven't been in love yet," Justin told *M Magazine*. "But I've felt love. It's a beautiful emotion that you can't really describe." Justin is looking forward to falling in love in the future, but he's enjoying being single and focusing on work for now!

So what's next for J.B.? Well, he's recorded *Part II* to *My World* to release in March 2010, and he can't wait to share it with his fans. Justin would love to record an album a year—or more if possible! But he does have to set aside time for school, music video shoots, concerts, appearances, and some downtime for friends and family! Justin is steadily working his way through his high school coursework and would love to go to college one day. He also wants to focus on songwriting and really growing as a musical artist.

Justin spent the end of 2009 making appearances on TV shows, award shows, and at malls. However, many of his appearances became so crowded with rowdy fans that some had to be cancelled. That so many people want to see him perform is still surprising to Justin, as he explained to reuters.com: "I've gained a lot more fans, and I'm able to travel a lot more. I went to the U.K. for the first time in the summer, and hundreds of girls came out to see me. I wasn't totally surprised because a lot of the people who comment on my YouTube videos are from overseas, but I still had no idea that many people would come." Justin and his record label are working on plans to take his act on tour both in the U.S. and around the world. So keep an eye out for tickets on sale at a concert hall near you!

Justin's career is just getting warmed up. Luckily for his fans, he's super cute and super talented and he has the drive every star needs to make it big. He's focusing on his music and his fans and he's set to become the biggest star of his generation. So stay tuned—Justin will be very busy over the next few years and you won't want to miss a thing from this talented cutie!

Name: Justin Drew Bieber
Nicknames: JBiebs, Bieber, Beebs
Birthday: March 1, 1994
Hometown: Ontario, Canada
Current Town: Atlanta, Georgia
Pet: A dog named Sam
Sibling: Half-sister Jazmyn
Height: 5'3"
Hobbies: Soccer, hockey, singing
Best Friend: Ryan Butler
Favorite Color: Blue
Favorite Food: Spaghetti and meatballs, tacos
Favorite Number: 6
Favorite Drink: Orange juice
Favorite Movies: The *Rocky* series
Favorite Dessert: Apple pie